Life According to Jade

Jade Brown

BookLeaf
Publishing

Presentation by *BookLeaf Publishing*

Web: www.bookleafpub.com

E-mail: info@bookleafpub.com

ISBN: 978-93-95969-66-6

First edition 2022

Dream Worlds

Night is the time to say goodbye to the past
It is the time to wish for sleep-all night, that lasts
It is the time to forget all your worries and troubles
It is the time to allow your dreams to bubble
So lay your head on your pillow tonight
And don't forget to hug your blanket really tight
 I wish you a very very good night

Nature is Born

Go outside,
Let your breath be stolen away,
find the forests,
Seek the seas,
Meditate on a mountain,
Mist covered from the morning,
We are nurtured by nature,
Born for the wild places,
We've no business in cities,
In buildings taller than trees can grow,
Go outside,
Begin living again.

Call on the Witches

I call to the Witches both near and far
No need to name you, you know who you are
Come dance with me by the firelight
Give praise to the Goddess

This full moon night
It doesn't matter where you are
Send your soul
It travels far

I will wait for you and the sun goes to rest
I will be truly blessed
Brothers
Sisters
Dance with me as I will it
So more if be

Family

This is my family bracelet,
Worn so others will see the blessings God has
granted,
Through our family,
With my Lord in the center,
To Him I give the glory,
The other gems tell the story of our family,Mom
and Dad set on each side,
Children in between,
A perfect circle.

My Flower

My flower is wonderful and sweet
She never leaves my side
She will always be planted deep inside my heart
My flower is a special friend
So wonderfully truthful too
My flower is a special friend
Like the one I have in you

The Pain in Your Heart

I see pain
I see need
I see liars
Thieves
Abusing power with greed
I had hope
I believed
I'm beginning to think I've been deceived

A Broken Heart

7

How do you mend a broken heart
Where do you begin
Where do you start
How do you face another day
What do you say

It's never easy
Getting back into the swing
There's no doubt it will take it's toll
You have to be strong and forge ahead
Then, things will start to roll

To Be a Good Friend

I will laugh when you laugh,
I will cry when you cry,
I will tell you you're lovely - that's no lie,
I will join you for lunch,
We'll share a dessert,
We'll catch up on gossip,
And dish all the dirt.

The Future

6th grade rushes on
The work grows harder
The days grow longer

But our friends help us on the way
As do the teachers
All friends together
Together as one we stand

The homework grows
The dances come
Grades rise and fall

Yes, it is fun to be educated
Inspiring people
Become inspired

The projects grow farther apart
As do the mistakes we make
Let's take a moment and think

Think back on our past
Recollect the experiences we have had
And will always cherish

I Want to be a Super Hero

When I was younger, I wanted to be struck by
lightening
I wanted to wake up a Super Hero
I wanted to fly, shoot lasers and heal rifts

I wanted to be the provider of miracles
Because I needed to be a hero
Because I needed miracles
Because a healer could fix all the breaks

I wanted to be struck by lightening
I would run into the rain
I would hold my wire hanger
I would call out to the sky
Please save my life!

The New Generation

Welcome to my generation
The teens are
The children lie
Our youth want to die-and we love our
good-byes

Where the girls are fat
And the boys are thin
We blame the cat
And do nothing but sin

Where the bullies are glorified
To Hell is personified
And those that hate it here
Aren't allowed to tell others their fears

So welcome to my generation
I hope you stay
Or you could join me
And we'll both run away

My Mother's Lullaby

Cast away your worries my dear
For tomorrow comes a new day
Hold to me, you've nothing to fear
Your dreams are not far away
As you lay your head and rest
May your dreams take over
My love
Listen close my son of the West
For your destiny lies above you
The world is cruel
There is a light that still shines
In the darkest days of our life
Hope is not lost
You can find your way
Think of me as you look to the sky
Child
Your future is bright
Your Father's blood is in your veins
I pray you will fight
For these lands will soon know your name

I Know a Place

I know a place
That is sound and safe for us
No need to hide or say good-bye
Leave them out
We'll run away

It'll be ok
We can chase waterfalls
Talk til my hair dries
Just lie on the sand
Each hand in hand in paradise

Cause we don't have long til we say "so long"
We can live in this lovely dream
It'll be my reality

I know a place that has no trace of us now
It's just a thought
Don't tell me I'm wrong

If I Could Ride a BIke

If I could ride a bike
I'd zoom around the world
With you sitting there behind me

I'd take you to places
Past several places
Just live and live

If I could sail a boat
I'd cruise across the seas
Sweet adventures for us

We'll be Jack and Jill
Just please don't let me go
I'd be nothing without you

When you call me
I'm drifting on clouds
Like I'm dreaming

But in the morning I'll wake up and see you stuck
with me
If only you knew what I would do for you
I would jump up and hold you so tightly

But I will never be able to do these things
So I'm just left imagining

True Love

To my one and only true love
You have given my life a dove
A dove being a sign of peace
It allows my true self to release

You helped me learn to be strong
And helped me keep it for so long
You are there when I cry
Even though I am shy

I feel complete with you
Making everyday feel like new
I am so happy to know that you love me
It fills my heart with glee

Your smile is absolutely breath taking
Just like your voice, it gets my heart pumping
You've made my life into a wonderful story

I hope it can be a story where we marry
I hope that our love blossoms further
And we can live happily, forever

A boy like you is one of a kind
Our love is strong when combined
Thank you for being my Valentine
Thank you for being mine

My Soul is Spirited Away

The birth of my spirit
A culmination of electrons
Hand picked to perfection
The literal spark of life

I mature and become wise
With the knowledge of God and morals
Given a conscience to heed a will to obey
Simplicity in form and purpose

Though I realize what's to come
I remember the lessons learned as I journey
onward
I leave this home to find a new dwelling

My spirit comes upon a body a rests
After its journey through time, I will see again
These days are momentarily forgotten
This is only the beginning of my life

The Shining Sun

The shining sun on a hot day of summer
We can spend time with one another
Swimming in the cool water
When the sun shines upon the water
You start to run around and it gets hotter
You play until the sun starts to go down
You wish it would never end

Blooming

Blooming red
Blooming blue
Out in the Spring
I'm thinking of you
Your wonderful eyes
Like and ocean view
When you speak, I get butterflies too
The way you smile
The way you dress
When it comes to you
I can't properly confess
Your beautiful skin
Your kind expression